© 2011 Marlon J. McGowan

Published by Jah X-El Publications

Edited and formatted by Jah X-El

Printed in the United States of America

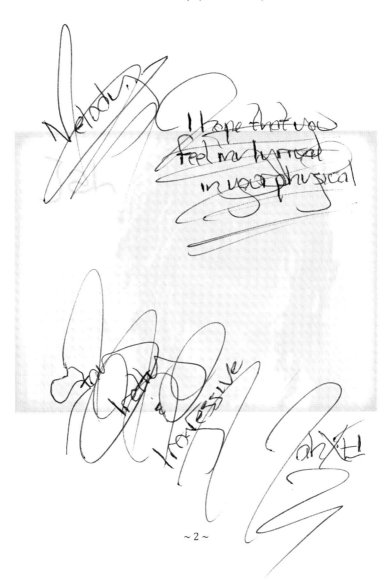

Thank God for my gift of creative writing...

...However way I poetically express myself, without His blessing, it would NOT be possible

Table Of Contents

"*Opening Thought*"

"*Thought*"

"*Thought*"

"Thoughts"

"Thought"

"Thought"

"Closing Thought"

DIG... "TRUTH SPEAK, GOOD CONVERSATION WHILE LAYING IN BED IS A POTENT FORM OF INTIMACY... PILLOW TALK... FOREPLAY IN THE FORM OF COMMUNICATION..." ~ JAH X-EL

Bo

Call me Bo...

...I'm bow

legged

I even
have
a bow
3rd leg...

...I swing
low

...Sweet
chariot

I swing to
the left,
how I
carry it...

...I'm
blessed

You can

measure
it...

...Or
simply
try it

I promise
I'll bow
your back
each time
I thrust
with it...

Flow Switch

...I'll slide one finger in, curve it

Bow it like a banana so that my fingertip can massage the spot
by your cervix...

...Lean forward and firmly press the tip of my tongue on your
clit

Take your hands out of my locs and put them behind your
head woman; I GOT THIS!!!

...Raise your damn hips!!!

Rotate them then grind on my bowed tongue while I give you

cunnilingus...

...Now you think you're ready to fuck Bo's bowed dick???

Suga Flow

Relax my dear

This will be
something
different here

Another form
of sexual cheer

Unlike none
you've
EVER read

Poetry the
likes of you'll
NEVER hear

Suga flow...

...Flow cool

Chasing
the cool...

...Fall
classic cool

October's weather

This is a
hardcore, freaky
writings on
and within your
walls until you're
spilling L.A. hot,
Detroit cool,
type flow

A poetic
flow to let
you know

Something about
you speaks
to me
SO dominant...

...I think
your legs
are crossing over

...Jah got
you wet

Legs re-open
wide...

Suga love
making
session

Chocolate erection

Ready to
dip inside
your flavorful
section

I'll write
a story
on the
page, which
is your
body, with
my tongue

The cream
from your
cookies being
the ink

I won't
just lick
you til
you cum...

...I'll lick
you till
you're numb

I'll lick you
till you're
babbling
incoherently
and rendered

temporarily
DUMB...

Vanilla Lady

Strawberry Girl

Mocha Woman

Imagine my
body movement's
volume while
pleasing you

...Various

Let me
inside you

...Experience

Seashore chills

Hear familiar
noises

...Sounds orgasmic

Seize the
pleasure

Explicit wildflower

Jah will
perform verbal

intercourse
on top
of the
forehead of
your inner cherry

Get it?

I'll whisper
dirty words
while nastily
assaulting you
with my
filthy tongue

Place your
mind in
a euphoric
submission hold

Send it up
in the attic...

...beyond
the skies

Dwell in
heaven with
other well
pleased souls

Speak to
me Suga

With sweaty
body language

Your suga
secretions will
have my dick
looking better
than a
Dunkin Stick

Then again,
your honey
glaze on
my lips will
have them
better moisturized
than Chapstick

...Suga

Inhale deeply
while I
orally indulge

...Suga

Strawberry scents
& apple plums

...SoOgaH

I'll be
peeking to

see you
peaking...

...As I'm
looking over
the peak of
your hips
while licking
your pink

Watching the
rise and
swell of
your breast...

Jah gives
Luther Vandross
type cunnilingus

...So Amazing!

Have your
heart racing

Skin flushed
and blazing

Scream my
name and
let me
know there's
NO other

I'll reward
you by
making you
DeAngelo moan

Shit...

...Damn

MOTHERFUCKER!!!

Dig... "Ladies, truth speak, watch your man thrust... Your legs spread, seeing his shaft glide, pile drive style, inside, is a must... Pistoning penis in and out of you until you erupt... Inner thighs and lips drenched until you watch him lick up what you've bust..." ~ Jah X-El

Ride

...My mouth
WILL ride
your curves

Navigate your
EVERY turn...

...Explore
your plateaus

My tongue
WILL hold
onto your
body's roads...

...Let me
steer my lips
over AND
through your
physical passage fast
or slow

Drive you like
a professional
to sexual
destinations
the previous
amateurs you
let ride could
NEVER go...

Touch

She said she
wanted to
grope me...

...I told her
that she
could if I can
touch her

With feels
that will
make her
feel violated...

...In a
good way

Like ordering
her to take
her panties
off in public...

...Dip off on
the side of

a building
and dip
into her so
that I can
get her
off in public

Violate her by
holding her...

...In a
masculine way

While
straddling one
of her legs
while she lays
on her side,
gripping her
cheeks firmly,
then pulling
her back
to meet
my thrusts...

...I told her
that I'll rub
her the
right way

She'll feel
the magic
in my touch...

...Johnny Gill
sex

Have her
continuously
moaning

my...

My

...MY

Dig… "Men, truth speak, with your woman, NOTHING wrong with morning tangles… Have her legs vertical, then parallel to the pillows… Leave them like Jello…" ~ Jah X-El

Calgon

You had a
difficult day?

You are more
than welcome
to jump in the
tub with me
and allow me to
stroke all your
stress away

Before you come
in, your clothes,
toss them away

What a
beautiful sight

You're just
as beautiful
as the day

you were born

You don't
need clothes

They don't do
you ANY justice
at all when
they are worn

You need
my touch
because I
can actually
hear your
body mourn

Calling to me

Candles lit

No lights tonight

It's time
to perform

Our body's
temperature
can help keep
this bath
water warm

I want to fit
your shape
to my physical,
and mold your
soft feminine
frame to
my hard
masculine form

Maybe recite
to you
a poem

Off the top
of my head
while I take
you to a sexual
peak by long
stroking inside

your valley
underwater; Yes,
my sex acts
will reconstruct
the norm

The evidence of
our lovemaking
will be in the
bathroom everywhere

I will rest
in peace on
top of you
and in between
your thighs,
my piece
will be
buried there

10 inches deep
inside of you,
all the way to
my pubic hair

10 inch strokes
of depth in
and out of
you while you
ride me, that
will make you
moan, talk
in tongues,
and swear

Before I stand
you up, get
behind you,
dip your back,
slide in deep,
and for 1
minute, just
hold it there

Reach between
your thighs,
place two
fingers on your
clit, and gently
massage it while

I stroke long,
slow, and deep
inside you while
I pull your hair

Jah's way of
taking YOU away,
because "Calgon"
could NEVER take
you there

Wet

When I start
tonguing you
down, It'll be
like river currents
are lapping at
your pussy

I will have
you releasing
flows that will
make the average
man drown, or
moisturize his
head to the
point that his
brain will be
soaked and his
dirty thoughts
are muddy

Let's get nasty

I can't think
of doing my

next piece
because I keep
imagining some
of you women
masturbating

Truth speak, I
can't piece
together new
pieces because
I have these
oral fixations

It's agitating

Trying to recite
poetry while
steady thinking

I'm hungry with
horniness and
there's so many
options on my
menu, but I'm
not into drive
through women

But, whomever
I end up with...

...My tongue
tides will be
pulling at
her center
like magnets

My mouth
maneuvers will
have her
screaming and
moaning...

"Jah, I need a levee"

...and ALL I'm
thinking is that
I'll simply use
my tongue
to dam this

DAMN THIS

I'll give you
aquafina flows,
running through
your panties
like tidal waves

You'll be so

soaked you'll
be lacing your
panties with 2
panty-liners,
biker shorts,
leggings, and
a pair of pants
just to make it
through the day

Your stream
will become a
slip and slide

Get use to
staying wet

Have extra
pairs of panties
on standby

Thinking of
Jah licking
your twa got
you melting

Icebergs create
less water

I'll make

you cum lakes

I've NEVER
been afraid
of deep
sea diving

Or putting
my face
in geysers

But, truth speak,
real pussy eaters
DON'T let our
words lead

We allow
our tongues
to guide us

Game Time

You can't just
dribble through
my thoughts...

...I'll pass
on that

I rather take
a shot at
making your
butt bounce...

...Cheeks
rebounding
off my hips as
I hit you
from the back

Its game time...

...A professional

pumper will
enter and fill
your arena

Tear down your
walls, dig up
feminine floors,
then lay down
my masculine
hardwood...

...My stroke
is pure

When Jah
shoots...

...Scores
of cum
is released

This is why
I would rather
ball you than
watch the

basketball
game on TV...

She Hate Me

You want
me inside
of you
until it feels
like I'm
waist deep?

You want
me to take
my Magnum
XXL filler
out of
the holster
and take it
off safety?

I have enough
length to
go swimming
in your
womanly pool
10 inches deep

I have 2 1/2
inches of
circumference
to make the
filling of
your feminine
opening
complete

And I'm
not an
inconsiderate
or selfish
sexual beast

My objective
is NOT to
hurt with
my size,
but to
allow YOU
to dictate
how much
of Lil' Jah
is needed
to please

So I'm
willing to
sway
wherever
your climax
seeking
crescendo
takes me

And I
can be
submissive,
so don't
be afraid
to throw
it on
me
aggressively

Talk to
me nasty

Cuss me
out during
our
lovemaking

like you
hate me

I've always
thought that
you were
the rose that
could crack
my concrete

And thoughts
of you have
had me
harder than
brick lately

So please
allow me
to stroke
inside you
until you're
whispering

"Oohh Jah,
you got me
leaking baby!"

I'm a sexual
thief and
I'll steal
your breath
with strokes
of depth
that will
leave you
unable to
speak lady

Star Trek (*The ATD Dedication*)

She wants me
to explore
the astronomy
that we share

To conduct a
scientific study
of matter...

...between our
inner and
outer spaces

Especially the
positions and
dimensions and
distribution of
our motion,
energy, and
the evolution
of our

celestial bodies

It's phenomenal
as space how
much we
care about
each other

She wants
to know how
we are
gravitationally
bound

Held in
orbit together

When our
bodies eclipse
during our
regular
mating rounds

She wants
thrusts in

and out
of her that
will break
the barrier
of sound

Rushing her
to climax

That's called
Supersonic Sex

She wants
me to
frolic around
her planets...

...and leave
new milky ways

between all
4 of her
supple planets...

Star-bursts bust

and leave us BOTH star struck
and star gazed

She wants me
to use my
miniature rocket
to invoke...

...cataclysmic
emotions inside
of her with
an infinite
number of long
deep strokes

She wants me
to gently
indulge in her
black hole with
various pace

An object whose
gravitational pull
is so strong
even light

can't escape

She wants
me to send
stellar winds
rushing through
her galaxy

Causing
outbursts of
stardust to
shoot into her,
out of me

We BOTH
discovering
simultaneously...

...that the
Big Bang Theory

truly exists...

Because we've
shared that

meteoric,
exploding feeling
together in
this great
sexual abyss

Which is why
she wants to
ALWAYS be
the greatest
terrestrial
form closest
to my heart

And I want
to give
her suns
and moons

That shine
as bright
as she is

While lying upon a
bed of stars

She is a
star with a
constellation
on her
mid section

Which makes
her illuminate
radiantly
in our
bedroom

Our cosmic
connection
should be
a lovers
Final Frontier

No object in
all the heavens
could cast a
shadow large

enough to
eclipse the solar
flares that

erupt whenever
we touch lips

It's amazing
to me how
our universe
is continually
expanding

She sends
me on
Star Trek trips

That's why this
exploration of
our universe
will forever be
never ending

Dig... "Truth speak, this SHOULD be remembered by EVERY dude BEFORE sexing... "She's BEFORE He's" when it comes to "releasing"..." ~ Jah X-El

Dig... "Ladies, truth speak, make your man orally please you until you orgasm SO hard it'll temporarily handicap BOTH your brain AND body..." ~ Jah X-El

Dig... "Truth speak, creative foreplay begins BEFORE the clothes come off and CAN include ANYTHING from phone sex to picture text..." ~ Jah X-El

Dig… "Truth speak, when it's understood that the tongue is actually a 9th finger during sex, the worth of touch CAN'T be described with mere words…" ~ Jah X-El

Dig… "Ladies, make your man make you make your legs make intersections… Then make him enter your section… Make him make you sex his erection…" ~ Jah X-El

Dig… "Truth speak, eye contact during intercourse is one of the smallest things you can perform that brings the biggest results…" ~ Jah X-El

Leggo

Leggo...

...Do
something
sexual

Make a
new position
called
"The Waffle"...

...Lay flat on
your stomach,
spread eagle

Get in
push-up
position
over you...

...Slide down,

forward and
in, then thrust;
pumping and
grinding until
my movements
create a
combined fluid
between us the
same texture
as the
ingredient in
an Eggo

Let's stack
our bodies
like a Lego...

...Pump
pleasurable
penis inside
you until
you let go

Until I
produce male

product that's
seminal...

...Baby, I'm
feeling you

So allow Jah
to fill you...

...Balls deep,
with the
width of a
tube from
a roll of
paper towel

Leggo...

...Test my
arsenal

I have a
10 millimeter,
NEVER
malfunctioning,

masculine
pistol...

...Ready to
piston in
and out
of you

Ready to
target, shoot
inside, and
murder your
womb...

The Invitation

...I want
you to be
my sexual
conquest

Become a
nymphomaniac
to my every
sexual request...

...I WON'T
stroke you
sweetly

My thrusts
will have
deeper
meaning...

...Meaning I'll
stroke deeper

than what
you're used
to feeling

Extend
your womb...

...I'll offend
the next man
following me
because he'll
think you
have a
bottomless
feminine tomb

I'm NOT
through...

...I'm called
King Cunnilingus
for the tongue
tricks I do

Come experience

Dig… "Consider making love… Not to be confused with simply having sex… Truth speak, making love enhances and is more intimate…" ~ Jah X-El

Planet Pleasure

I have my
own dialect
of love
for her

It can ONLY
be spoken
during foreplay,
when my
persona takes
off on our
sexual trip

Her sweetness
coats my lips

...I become

"Cunning the Linguist"

True master
of tongue

She inspires

me to lift
a glass
of moscato
to propose
a toast

"To oral copulation"

My seduction
method

With it, I'll
speak to her
body as if
it is my
native language

She'll be
hypnotized
by my
hallucinogenic
labia
stimulating
drug

A tempestuous,
tantalizing,
tantric oral
experience

Highly charged
pleasure currents

Shakes,
quakes
and quivers

Her moans
providing
aural
confirmation
of her
pleasure

I'll have
her anticipating
a thousand
foot drop

Climbing higher
as she
reaches her
climatic peak

Forget the
westside of
Heaven where
I'm from

She and
I will
be spinning
galaxies together

Holding planets
in form

Spiritually
activating
one another's
souls

Spiriting
through
the
dimensions

I'll be
sending her
parched
vaginal corridor
into twatiotic
ecstasy

Blessing her
with divine
orgasms

Leaving her
nothing to
do but
grab hold
of my
locs as
if clinging
to life
during this
sensexual
tropical storm

And on
this rapturous
route

With her
crescendo
reaching
fever pitch

I'll enter
her geometric
gateway to
the cosmos
with euphoric
strokes from
several
inches of

mathematics

THEN, we'll
continue our
spiritual hitch

Until like
a broken
fire hydrant...

...Together
we climax

Our
simmering
love
explodes in
a mix
of our
penal and
vaginal
liquids

Creating a
sexual baptism
of juices
seemingly
enough to
immerse

and drown
our souls

La petite morte
on our personal
planet of pleasure

My death-bed
and heaven,
found between
her legs; it
doesn't get
any better

Ms. Observer

Because you're
intrigued, you
now have my
absolute devotion

Every figment of
my imagination
focused on your
erotic inquires,
speculations, and
flirtatious motions

You want to
watch me feast
on highly defined
feminine lines?

Ms. Observer?

You want to be
an eye witness to
Jah The Sexual Conquer

as he, with his tongue,
accentuate the bold
curves of a woman's
anatomical dimensions?

I'm admitting...

Your desires has the
extension of my
lower body attentive

Lady, be
my peeping
submissive

I'll reward your
compliance with
abstract erotic images

A plethora of pussies
being pleased in
provocative positions

A conglomerate of
nymphs with amorous
characteristics that

can be forged
or licked into
"cum"posure until
saliva and sperm
creates a melting pot
of molten emulsions

Jah meets Ms. Observer

Jah will have her
working her fingers
in and out of
herself like a piston

Watching my sexual
acts on another
woman will
have her cummin' so
hard she'll be pissin'

Squirt Ms. Observer...

...While moaning,

"Jah, DICK HER!!!"

Your eyes are
like prisms of
visible light reflecting
chocolate spectrum's
of lasciviousness
inside your cornea

They display a
wantonness for
the sweet
chocolate bar
penetrating between
this woman's legs
as I'm stroking her

Breathing for you
has become an
aroused labor

Sexual delirium has
you reaching ahead
to embrace our
fornicating postures

The way I'm
thrusting in and

out of this
woman has you

feverishly wishing
she was NOT doing
Jah, but Jah was
doing YOU,
Ms. Observer

That OTHER Shit (*Short Sensual Shit*)

...Nothing AT
ALL subliminal
about what
I'll do to you

I DON'T
got to
B More careful...

...I speak,
you KNOW
who I'm
talking to

I issue orders,
you know
EXACTLY
what to do...

...Bend over

Bless the walls
with your

hands presence...

...Miss
them pants

Around one of
your ankles is
where your panties
will be resting...

...Your legs
WILL be splitting

Then I'll deliver
a hard package
where your legs
are intersecting...

...I bet when
you walk past
construction men,
male monuments
will be erecting

Make them
want to jack
their hammers...

...Nail you

You're a
brick-house, but
you can ALWAYS
use some
good wood...

...Jah be on
that OTHER
lyrical shit

Lyrics that will
make a lesbian
consider a
back switch...

...I can motivate
Kelly to lick
Beyonce's clit

I can degenerate
Ms. Degeneres
and make her
want to suddenly
suck dick...

Dig… "Dude, truth speak, impregnate your woman with climaxes… Have her expecting bundles of joy… She'll birth multiple orgasms for you…" ~ Jah X-El

Restaurant

I want to
be your
restaurant...

...I'll prepare
and give
you healthy
servings of
tube steak and
tossed salad

Whip you with
strokes from
my male
whisk until
you cream...

...Sip your
feminine wine
from the
chalice between
your legs

Gobble girl
gravy from
your goblet...

...Let my
chocolate bar
plow into your
strawberry fields

I'll churn out
an orgasm in
YOU that will
make **ME**
produce masculine
vanilla butter...

...Then part
your thighs
and let me
lick the leftovers

I'll call
THAT our
"Neopolitan Mixture"...

I Remember

...Her sugar
walls had my
tongue twisted

like a Twizzler

Left swirls
around her
pearl like a
Candy Cane
when I
licked her...

...Until I had
her begging
me to dig deep
into her Kit Kat
with my King
Size Snickers

I Ponder

When I lick
your cheeks,
my saliva will
leave a
candy glaze...

...Part your
lips, slide my
peppermint
stick between
your cakes

Pull out
after plentiful
pumps...

...Spray and
spread masculine
honey on
your buns

I call that
Hostess Fornication...

...I have pork
that will have
you wanting
to part your
thighs like
a wishbone

My bone
will have
you wishing...

...Wish bone
like Jah's was
given by your
mans bone

Wishful thinking...

…My food for
thought will
make you have
hungry pussy
pangs; I can
hear it growling

I got enough
meat to store
in your
feminine freezer;
open up and
start packing

Dining on Jah
will keep you
from starving…

…You ready to
start snacking?

Never Will I

We would take
long morning walks
in the sun

Have beautiful,
bountiful conversations

Speaking from the heart

But end our night
with sweaty bodies
from lovemaking

That SHOULD
be us...

...Yet, she
DOESN'T exist

But, there should
be a book
of her and I

First chapter

beginning with
alluring scribes

Fill it with
erotic verses

Of how I
would nibble from
her peach plot

Take bites of
her apple bottom

Indulge in
her cantaloupes

Lick and sip the
creaminess of
her vanilla float

Right after I taunt
her "little man" with
my banana, in
her womanly boat

She WILL moan

Vocalize her
pleasure like
Nina Simone

She'll harmonize like
Thuggish Ruggish Bone

...on bone...

While I spit poetic
styles between her
sultry thighs until she's
sitting on my
tongue as if on her
very own throne

She can be my
female Rakim, fiening
for my Microphone

Check 1 - 2

Take away two...

...Add zero

That's 10...

...Inside of YOU

Intrigued?

I'M SURE!!!

;-) Wink - Wink ;-)

I would carve
her name...

...on the
inner walls

of her
feminine cavern...

...with my masculine
digging and
excavating tools

That would be

"Groove Theory"

And I want her
womb to know me
like "John Holmes"
and "Vanessa Del Rio"
in X rated
films: Legendary

I NEVER want
her to forget me

Forget me not

Even after I
climax and drip drip
onto her
soft landscape
masculine raindrops

My lovemaking
make her
have downfalls

She WILL fall down

To her knee's

She or me

Either her or I,
either one,
eager to please

In 69 ways

I got a flute, that's
ready to blow...

...She has a faucet

that's ready to flow

Upon my thick,
lengthy intro

...Enter slow

Firm, but
shallow...

...Short, hard,
thrusts hitting
different spots
when pumping
in various angles

Then speed
the tempo...

...going deeper
with more strokes

Until her inner
muscles squeeze,
contract, then
let go...

SPLASH

Waterfalls

NEVER will I…

NOT

…leave her in

Puddles, puddles

And after wards,
lick from her
bowl her
orgasmic residuals

Sounds good?

I know…

Too bad "she"
and my fantasies
aren't MORE
than just wishful

DIG... "TRUTH SPEAK, GOOD SEX IS MENTAL... IT'S THE TYPE OF SEX THAT HAS AN INDIVIDUAL EXPERIENCING PHYSICAL AROUSAL JUST FROM PAST REMEMBRANCES..." ~ JAH X-EL

Made in the USA
Charleston, SC
16 June 2013